SHUTTING DOWN BULLIES

SHUTTING DOWN
BULLIES AT HOME

Jessica Shaw

rosen publishing's
rosen
central

New York

Published in 2020 by The Rosen Publishing Group, Inc.
29 East 21st Street, New York, NY 10010

Library of Congress Cataloging-in-Publication Data

Names: Shaw, Jessica, 1972– author.
Title: Shutting down bullies at home / Jessica Shaw.
Description: First edition. | New York : Rosen Publishing, 2020. | Series: Shutting down bullies |
Includes bibliographical references and index.
Identifiers: LCCN 2019007518| ISBN 9781725347045 (library bound) | ISBN 9781725347038
(paperback)
Subjects: LCSH: Bullying—Prevention—Juvenile literature. | Parent and child—Juvenile literature.
Classification: LCC BF637.B85 S57 2020 | DDC 302.34/3—dc23
LC record available at https://lccn.loc.gov/2019007518

Manufactured in the United States of America

Some of the images in this book illustrate individuals who are models.
The depictions do not imply actual situations or events.

CONTENTS

Introduction

From classrooms and playgrounds to homes, workplaces, and cyberspace, bullying is a far-reaching, serious problem that affects many. Bullying isn't a new issue, but the ways in which people are bullied have evolved over time, making it even more difficult to stomp out. No one is immune to bullying, regardless of his or her perceived successes or failures, perfections or imperfections, or socioeconomic status. As antibullying campaigns have gained ground, many celebrities have come forward to share their own personal stories of childhood bullying and to speak up for other victims of bullying.

Michelle Trachtenberg, an actress who had recurring roles in popular shows such as *Gossip Girl* and *Buffy the Vampire Slayer*, endured vicious bullying during her high school years. Her ribs were fractured when she was thrown down a flight of stairs, and her nose was broken when she was punched in the face. Actress, businesswoman, and founder of The Honest Company, Jessica Alba was bullied so badly in high school that she ate lunch in the nurse's office and her dad walked her in to school each morning for protection. Award-winning actor, singer, and producer Hugh Jackman recalls years of bullying from an older brother, who repeatedly called him a sissy because of his interest in dancing. Sidharth Malhotra, a successful actor from India, was bullied and physically abused by an older brother. All of these people were victimized by bullies and went on to achieve amazing success in life. When more people speak out against

Despite years of teasing from his brother, Hugh Jackman continued to pursue his passion for the performing arts!

bullying, and are open about their struggles, hopefully fewer people will be forced to endure it.

Bullying that happens at home is perhaps the most traumatic of all. Home should be a safe place—a refuge from challenges and troubles faced elsewhere. When bullying occurs at home, whether by a friend, acquaintance, or family member, it is still bullying and should not happen. There is help, hope, and healing for anyone enduring this type of bullying.

CHAPTER ONE

Bullies, Bystanders, and victims

Often, when bullying occurs, there are others present. Bullies, bystanders, and victims all play a role in determining the outcome of a bullying encounter and the likelihood of similar encounters happening in the future.

WHAT IS BULLYING?

Sometimes bullying goes unreported because the victim is unsure of whether or not he or she has actually been bullied. There are several specific elements present when bullying occurs. First, there must be an intention to control or harm someone, either physically or emotionally. True bullying doesn't happen by accident. The actions or words are deliberate and cruel. Next, the hurtful behavior is repetitive, rather than a one-time thing. Lastly, there is either a real or perceived imbalance of power. This might mean the person targeted is smaller in size or that he or she feels in some way socially inferior. Bullying can happen in any number of settings, including at home. There is a difference between bullying and random, unkind behavior.

Young children express their thoughts unfiltered, meaning they often don't always stop to think—or don't yet realize—that certain comments could be hurtful to someone. This is not bullying. It's nice when all members of a household, class, or peer group are wholly inclusive, but there will be times when someone is excluded from a group or activity. Unless the purpose of the exclusion is to make the person feel bad, this type of exclusion is not necessarily bullying. Arguments and disagreements happen and usually do not rise to the level of bullying, unless one party is clearly being malicious or not letting the other talk. Similarly, teasing that is meant as a harmless joke

Though scary and unacceptable behavior, a one-time physical assault does not necessarily constitute bullying. However, if the same person repeatedly targets someone, it definitely rises to the level of bullying.

is sometimes not bullying. But if the teasing becomes hurtful, it's important to speak up to stop it.

THE ROLE OF BULLYING BYSTANDERS

Bullying bystanders are the people present, witnessing an act of bullying. According to researchers, in up to 85 percent of bullying incidents, there are bystanders. Bystanders can be divided into five categories, according to the choice they make.

- **Outsiders** are bystanders who watch someone being bullied and do nothing. Kids who identify with the victim and want the bullying to stop might be afraid to get involved, either because they fear the bully will target them or because they fear being seen as a snitch if they go to an adult.

- **Ringleaders** are bystanders who have used their social standing to bring about the incident between the bully and the victim. Even though they aren't directly bullying the victim, they are responsible for working behind the scenes, putting the events into motion.

- **Associates** are those who are helping the bully in some way, sometimes because they are afraid of the bully. They might restrain a victim or serve as a lookout during the bullying.

- **Reinforcers** laugh or make comments that further encourage and empower the bully. They are a huge part of the problem, and their positive reinforcement is one of the main reasons that bullies continue to victimize others.

- **Defenders** are bystanders who actually intervene to try to stop the bullying and comfort and help the victim.

Feelings such as loneliness, sadness, fear, and insecurity are often factors in bullying, for both the victim and the bully.

ALL ABOUT BULLIES

There are certain characteristics that many bullies have in common, no matter how they engage in bullying. At first glance, all bullies might seem simply mean-spirited, cruel, and lacking empathy. Often, however, what bullies are feeling inside does not align with what they are exhibiting through their words or actions. Many bullies have emotional issues, such as anxiety or depression, which they don't know how to deal with properly. They often lack social skills, sometimes because of their emotional issues, and may find it very difficult to make and maintain friendships. Frequently, bullies have, themselves, been the victims of bullying. Some people turn that experience around, vowing to make sure others around them are never treated badly, but others let the frustrations and hurt feelings build up inside and eventually take it out on others. Some bullies act out because they are desperate for attention, either because they feel neglected by family members or because they are struggling to make friends. One, or a combination of

Bullies lack social skills and healthy coping mechanisms. When they are upset, hurt, or frustrated, they tend to engage in bullying behaviors.

any, of these issues can make a person feel insecure. A lack of self-confidence is usually what most bullies feel on the inside, even while acting like they are sure of themselves and in control. Lastly, some bullies truly do not realize how hurtful their words or actions are to others. In those situations, the bullying stops once the bully learns how devastating the effects of his or her behaviors have been.

BYSTANDERS AND VICTIMS OF BULLYING

In order to feel powerful and in control, bullies often go after their targets in front of bystanders. After all, if no one else sees bullies exerting control over their victims, how will they attract attention or put their dominance on display? The power trip that bullies seem to enjoy sometimes relies on an audience. Bullies might want others—peers on a playground, other children at home, or even other adult bystanders—to see how much power they have. When bystanders are present, their actions, or lack thereof, can make a huge impact on the outcome, for both the victim and the bully. Victims of bullying are often quiet and shy and are sometimes targeted for those very reasons. Research about the victims of bullying has also shown that they tend to be sensitive, may be upset or frightened easily, lack large, supportive friend groups, and often blame themselves for incidents, especially when the bullying is happening at home. Nothing could be further from the truth, though; the only one at fault for bullying is the bully!

CHAPTER TWO

Bullies at Home: Siblings

Disagreements and jealousy are common between siblings, regardless of age or gender. Brothers fight with brothers, sisters fight with sisters, and sisters fight with brothers when sibling rivalry rears its ugly head. Sometimes, however, when harsh words or actions are continuously initiated by one sibling against another, there is more than sibling rivalry going on. Siblings can be bullies, too.

LIVING WITH A BULLY

While it's a commonly held belief that the vast majority of bullying takes place at school, research shows that sibling bullying is as much as three times more common than school bullying. Between one-third and one-half of children under age eighteen are involved in sibling bullying. Like other forms of bullying, sibling bullying occurs when the negative behaviors are exhibited by someone who has real or perceived power over another, are intentionally hurtful, and are repetitive in nature. A 2014 study of 350 students revealed that bullying by siblings causes higher levels of stress, anxiety, and depression than peer bullying. Bullying is more likely to occur between siblings close in age, and the instances of sibling bullying tend to increase with family size.

Parents can find it difficult to distinguish between sibling rivalry and bullying. Bad behavior between siblings is often chalked up to the notion that "kids will be kids." Unfortunately, adopting that attitude may keep children who are being bullied from turning to the adults in the home for help. No parent wants to believe that one of his or her children is a bully, but a bullied child who can't turn to a parent for help is only going to feel more anxious, depressed,

An older sibling should be someone to trust and look up to, not someone who frequently causes hurt, fear, or anger.

and stressed about the situation. Ideally, if a parent thinks it's possible that one child is being bullied by another, action will be taken immediately to end the bullying. The fighting should not be ignored, and the sibling who has been hurt should be shown empathy and understanding, while the sibling who is bullying should be held accountable and helped to understand just how hurtful bullying behaviors are. Extra supervision along

13

with modeling kind, empathetic behaviors and giving both siblings healthy strategies to deal with their emotions and disagreements can help put an end to sibling bullying.

LASTING EFFECTS ON FAMILIES

There is no question that bullying is a universal problem that touches people all over the world. In 2018, a series of articles about sibling bullying was published in an Irish newspaper. Soon after, dozens of readers reached out with their own heartbreaking stories of being bullied by siblings. A common

A dysfunctional sibling relationship can leave long-lasting emotional scars and cause severe psychological problems.

thread throughout many of the stories was that the parent, or parents, in the home either did nothing to stop the abuse, or, in the worst cases, actually condoned and encouraged the bullying behavior.

One woman who was the youngest of six siblings wrote about the bullying she endured from an older brother. Her mother pretended the abuse wasn't happening, while her father was physically abusive towards her brother. Her brother, in turn, physically abused her, frequently punching her with all his might.

A man who was bullied by a brother who was four years older than him wrote, "In my home, there was no escape. My tormentor was there every day waiting for me." He was locked inside his bedroom for hours at a time and threatened with violence. He was repeatedly belittled and told that he was ugly. But his brother was a good student and was very well-behaved away from home, and so was never held accountable for bullying him.

Another man who was bullied by his brother was told by his parents, "You're bigger than him. Hit him back!" That was the extent of his parents' involvement in the situation. The verbal and physical bullying by his brother continued for nearly two decades, when, finally, he was able to leave home.

One story tells of a boy who bullied his younger brother for fifteen years, beginning when the younger brother was only a toddler. The bullying brother peed in his brother's bed, destroyed his personal possessions, filled his shoes with honey, and tormented him on a daily basis. The younger brother remembers the day his tormenter finally moved out to go to college as "the best day of my childhood."

Reaching out to talk to someone about a sibling bully is an important and helpful step when trying to heal emotional wounds and rebuild healthy relationships.

The resentment of siblings who are bullied can last well into adulthood, often alienating family members and leaving victims with lingering feelings of anger and depression. A 2014 study with more than 6,000 children found that being bullied by a sibling at age twelve doubled the odds of depression, anxiety, and self-harm by age eighteen. A study from the University of Warwick in 2018 found that kids involved in frequent sibling bullying were two to three times more likely to develop a psychotic disorder later in life.

MYTHS AND FACTS ABOUT BULLYING

Myth: Bullying happens only in schools.

Fact: Bullying happens in all types of settings. In the workplace, between employees or managers, within social groups, such as in sports teams, youth groups, or recreational clubs, online, through text messages or social media, and in the home, when one sibling bullies another, one adult bullies another, or an adult bullies a child.

Myth: Bullying always involves physical violence.

Fact: There are many types of bullying, and physical bullying is only one. Verbal bullying, such as name-calling, humiliation, threats, intimidation, and insults, can cause lasting psychological damage. Likewise, repeatedly stealing or destroying someone's property or excluding someone from a group or activity are also forms of bullying.

Myth: Bullying is a normal part of growing up.

Fact: There is nothing normal or okay about bullying. Left unchecked, bullying behaviors get worse, and victims of bullies can suffer extreme physical or psychological damage that lasts a lifetime.

Bullies at Home: Adults

In many ways, bullying that happens at home is more devastating than bullying that happens at school or within organized youth groups and events. Bullying by a brother or sister can be unrelenting and often destroys the love and trust that should be a natural part of a sibling relationship. Even worse, though, is being bullied by a parent or other adult in the home.

FEELING BULLIED BY A PARENT

So what exactly is bullying by a parent? Part of a parent's job is to be a disciplinarian, often saying things their kids don't want to hear—especially the word "no"—and, when necessary, doling out some type of punishment or explaining the consequences for certain actions. Parents aren't perfect, so naturally there will be times when they don't interpret a situation correctly or perhaps use a punishment that seems too harsh. Setting and enforcing rules, implementing reasonable punishments, denying certain freedoms, and telling a child he or she needs

When parents say something negative, they should think about whether the words are meant only to hurt, or if they are actually intended to help, guide, or teach.

to improve upon some aspect of his or her day-to-day life does not typically constitute bullying by a parent. However, there are many things parents should provide for their children, and if they aren't doing so or if they are taking punishments too far, they may be bully parents.

Some basic needs that parents should be providing for their children include food, drink, shelter, education, physical and emotional support, a safe and healthy environment, and love. There are two distinct types of bullying that a child can endure from a parent: physical bullying and emotional bullying. Both are very hurtful. Physical bullying includes actions such as hitting, kicking, or using an object to inflict pain. Physical bullying also includes depriving a child of physical needs, such as denying a meal or restricting a child from using the toilet or being able to wash as a form of punishment. These are the actions of a bully. Emotional bullying makes a child feel embarrassed, humiliated, or fearful. Examples of emotional parental bullying include threatening physical harm; name-calling or insulting, especially in front of others; preventing social interaction for long periods of time; demanding perfection; allowing the child to witness drug use, crime, or violence in the home; and making hurtful, negative comments related to a child's gender, sexual orientation, appearance, skills, intelligence, or social status. Bully parents engage in some or all of the above actions repeatedly.

Parents who bully do so for a variety of reasons. Often, they were bullied themselves as children, possibly by a parent. In these cases, the parents might not recognize that they are being a bully. If they were raised by parents who engaged in bullying behaviors or bullied as a substitute for discipline, they might believe that what their parents did—and what they are doing to their children—is normal parenting. Some bully parents are currently being bullied themselves. Workplace bullying happens way too often, just like other types of bullying. A cruel, demanding boss or an unrelenting, vicious coworker can cause a buildup of anger, resentment, and frustration in a parent, who, in turn, goes home each night and takes it out on a child. Another situation that sometimes leads to a parent bullying a child is when the parent is bullied by his or her spouse and feels betrayed, angry, and help-less to stop it. When parents in that situation bully their chil-dren, they are creating a cycle of abuse within the family. Though some bully parents do not rec-ognize or understand that they are being a bully, that doesn't excuse the behavior. Parents are expected to protect their chil-dren, not become their tormen-tors. In some cases, bully par-ents do realize that what they're doing isn't right, but they either don't care or don't have the self-control or emotional intel-ligence to stop. Whatever the influences behind these types of behaviors, the children of bully parents are left with the difficult task of seeking help to put an end to what's going on at home.

If parents repeatedly engage in hurtful behaviors, it's important to communicate—with them or with another trusted adult—about the negative impacts of their words or actions.

FEELING BULLIED BY OTHER ADULTS IN THE HOME

Sometimes, the bully at home isn't a sibling or a parent. A caretaker, such as a babysitter, could be the bully. Whether the caretaker is an older teenager or an adult, authority figures who use their temporary position of authority to bully must be

BULLYING BEHAVIORS BETWEEN ADULTS

When a parent is being mistreated by his or her spouse or partner, that parent might question whether or not it rises to the level of bullying or abuse. The following actions and behaviors indicate that there is bullying going on in a relationship:

Physical violence: There is no question that physically aggressive behavior is abuse. This is one of the most dangerous types of bullying.

Name-calling: This includes cursing at someone and using derogatory terms, but also includes using words such as "idiot," "stupid," "fat," or "worthless."

Threats: Threatening to harm someone physically, or in other ways that would be hurtful, is bullying.

Controlling behaviors: Preventing another adult from going out, accepting calls, having friends, working outside the home, driving, eating, or wearing certain clothes is bullying.

None of these behaviors is normal or healthy, and all are warning signs that it is time to end the relationship. Kids who witness a parent being bullied are more likely to engage in bullying behaviors themselves and to think that bullying is OK.

corrected. First and foremost, caretakers should ensure the children they are caring for are safe from harm. If, instead, they engage in name-calling, teasing, carrying out harsh punishments, or using controlling behaviors that go beyond enforcing the rules the parent has specified, they have become bullies rather than caretakers. Other adults in the home who could be bullies include relatives such as grandparents, aunts, or uncles. If a relative says something hurtful without realizing it, that is not bullying. However, anyone who inadvertently says something that makes a person feel embarrassed or upset needs to know that the comment was hurtful. Sometimes it happens because a word or phrase that was used frequently when he or she was growing up is no longer considered benign. Once a person knows better, he or she shouldn't repeat the offending word or phrase. If, on the other hand, a relative is intentionally causing harm or distress with either actions or words, there is no excuse for it. No one has the right to bully another member of the family. The same rules apply for any adults who may be staying as a houseguest. Being a friend of the family also does not give someone the right to be a bully to any member of the family and bullying, in fact, should be a one-way ticket out the door.

BULLYING IN FOSTER AND STEPFAMILIES

Unfortunately, bullying is even more common in foster families and stepfamilies. Families that have been brought together under unconventional circumstances are likely dealing with more than their fair share of stressors. Families that are blended together tend to be larger, on average. The kids who have been brought together may not know each other well, and up until that point, may have been raised in very different settings,

Blended families often struggle with forming healthy sibling relationships and are at higher risk of bullying within the home.

with very different rules and expectations. Suddenly, the family unit changes. Even if it changes for the better, change is still difficult. Feelings of jealousy or resentment can sometimes lead to bullying in the family. To further complicate the issue, both the adults and the children in the home may take sides when someone complains of bullying. There is a lot of pressure to make the new family work. No matter the makeup of a family, no one should have to put up with bullying. Finding someone to help stop the bullying and navigate the rough waters that can hit any family is crucial.

CHAPTER FOUR

Relational Bullying

Relational bullying is common, especially among girls. It is a type of bullying that involves one person trying to boost his or her own social standing while hurting someone else's social standing as well as his or her self-esteem and sense of well-being. It can happen in any setting. Relational bullying is not as easy to recognize as verbal or physical bullying, but can be just as damaging.

WHEN FRIENDS BECOME BULLIES

Relational bullies are sneaky and often go undetected. They present themselves as friends and target those who have a strong need for acceptance and friendship. For some people, it's not easy to make friends. This is especially true for those who are new to an area, socially awkward, shy, economically disadvantaged, or seen as different in some way. When bullies sense that others are unsure of themselves and desperate for companionship, they can use that insecurity and desperation to control and manipulate them.

The following is an example of relational bullying that might occur at home: Sidney is nice to her friend Jenna at school, where they are both good students. Each day after school, Sidney goes home with Jenna until her mom gets home from work. For some reason, Sidney acts very differently while at Jenna's house. She repeatedly criticizes the way Jenna has decorated her room, tells Jenna her house is way too small, always insists on choosing what they watch or play, and threatens to tell Jenna's parents about the boy she likes at school if she doesn't get her way. It's very difficult to understand why a friend

It's very difficult to accept or understand why someone who is supposed to be a friend is actually being a bully.

would become a bully when the setting changes. It's even more difficult to confront friends who bully in this way because they will again act nice when they want or need to. In this case, Sidney is actually lonely and envious of Jenna's home and family. Her mom is a single parent who had to take on a second job, so she isn't around much. They live in a small, cramped apartment, and she dreams of having a bedroom like Jenna's someday. Under these circumstances, Sidney's feelings are understandable. But instead of being honest with Jenna about how she is feeling, she lashes out at her. She has become a bully and is driving away a friend who could offer her support and understanding during a difficult time. Every time Sidney comes over, Jenna feels worse about herself.

WHEN FRIEND GROUPS GANG UP

Dealing with a friend-turned-bully is tough, but the pain and embarrassment can be even worse when friends gang up on another friend. Consider the following example of relational bullying: fourteen-year-old Amy just moved to a new state. She has a unique sense of style and her clothes stand out from most of the other teens in her new town. While taking a walk with her mom, she meets Maria, Kate, and McKenna, who live in her neighborhood. They smile and have a friendly conversation with Amy. Amy invites them over to her house the next day, and they readily accept her invitation, though Amy thinks she sees Maria looking her up and down, then glancing at Kate and McKenna and rolling her eyes. The next day, when her new friends arrive, they take turns commenting on her "weird" clothes and

When friends suddenly and repeatedly treat one member of the friend group unfairly, they are being bullies, not friends.

"boyish" haircut. They have made her feel insecure in her own home, and Amy's feelings are hurt, but she's desperate to have friends with whom she can celebrate her birthday the following weekend. She invites them all to her birthday party, and they tell her they will be there. When the big day rolls around, none of the girls show up. When Amy next sees them, they tell her they all went to a movie together instead. Then, they walk off, giggling, with a promise to invite Amy to the movies next time, if she dresses in "normal" clothes. Clearly, these girls are not Amy's friends. They are bullying her by excluding her and ridiculing her for her clothing and style choices. They have purposely been misleading Amy, are attempting to put conditions on their friendship, and are laughing at her expense.

Some individuals and groups bully by exclusion, and others by exerting power over someone. Conditional friendships are not real friendships. If one friend expects another to dress, talk, or act a certain way as a condition of the friendship, it's time to walk away. A friend who repeatedly makes someone feel bad,

PINK SHIRT DAY

In 2007, in the Canadian province of Nova Scotia, a ninth-grade boy was being bullied for wearing a pink shirt. Two older students, Travis Price and David Shepherd, knew the bullying was wrong and wanted to help put a stop to it. They went to a discount store and purchased fifty pink tank tops. That evening, they sent out a message to classmates, organizing a protest against bullying. The next morning at school, they handed out the pink shirts, which everyone wore in solidarity with the boy who had been bullied. When the bullied boy saw everyone in pink shirts, Price said, "It looked like a huge weight had been lifted off his shoulders." The bullies never bothered him again, and the compassionate gesture grew into a worldwide annual antibullying event. In 2018, nearly 180 countries participated in Pink Shirt Day, sending a strong message that bullying will not be tolerated!

physically or emotionally, or acts as if he or she is the leader in the friendship, clearly does not know how true friendship works.

CYBERBULLIES: WHEN HURTFUL WORDS FOLLOW YOU HOME

Cyberbullying is the use of technology to bully someone and gives bullies a way to hurt people even when they are at home alone. Social media is a fact of life, as are smartphones, email, and text messaging. Using any or all of these outlets, bullies can torment, intimidate, and humiliate their victims. Most teens,

Words on a screen can hurt just as much as spoken words, and, unfortunately, can be shared with many others quickly and easily.

and even many preteens, now have cell phones and email addresses. It's fairly easy to get someone's phone number and email address, either by simply asking others or by using an online search tool. Through texting, emailing, or online social media, bullies can send an unrelenting stream of cruel or threatening text messages or share embarrassing pictures or criticism. Remember that a bully's words, whether in person or on a screen, are meant to be hurtful and should not be taken to heart. As with other forms of bullying, cyberbullying should be reported to a trusted adult.

CHAPTER FIVE

Confronting and Conquering Bullying

When home is no longer a sanctuary from bullies, victims can feel helpless and hopeless. In the end, though, bullies don't win! More and more, the tables are turning on bullies, and they are realizing that today's society finds bullying behaviors unacceptable.

STATISTICS ON BULLYING

The Parent Advocacy Coalition for Educational Rights's (PACER) National Bullying Prevention Center has collected and compiled statistical data from a number of recent studies and surveys on bullying. Unfortunately, more than 20 percent of students report that they have been bullied. Another study found that 35 percent of students have either been bullied or have been the bully. When asked why they were bullied, the reasons most often given by victims included physical appearance, gender, disability, race/ethnicity, religion, and sexual orientation. Of LGBTQ+ students, 74 percent report being verbally bullied, and 36 percent report being physically bullied. Only about 20 to 30 percent of those who are bullied report it to an adult. Bullying at home is even more prevalent than school bullying, and many of the same attributes of a victim are targeted, whether at home or at school.

There are many people and organizations available to help victims shut down bullies and overcome the trauma they've endured.

THE TRAGIC EFFECTS OF BULLYING

The effects of bullying are far-reaching and long-lasting. Kids who are bullied by their peers have an increased risk of anxiety, difficulty sleeping, depression, and poor performance in school. Those involved in bullying, whether as the bully or as the target of bullying, are more likely to suffer from a variety of mental health issues and behavior problems. According to a 2016 study by the National Center for Educational Statistics, 19 percent of kids reported that bullying had negatively impacted how they felt about themselves, 14 percent said bullying negatively impacted their schoolwork and their relationships with friends and family, and 9 percent indicated their physical health was negatively impacted by bullying.

In the case of kids who are bullied by a parent, it's often a pattern that repeats itself, and they become bully parents themselves. They also frequently have trouble maintaining relationships as adults, have low self-esteem, greater fear of failure, and are prone to self-destructive behavior such as disordered eating, self-harm, and alcohol or drug abuse. Kids who endure bullying by a parent often exhibit aggressive behavior, and 80 percent of those who have suffered ongoing physical abuse by a parent develop some type of mental disorder.

STRATEGIES WHEN BEING BULLIED

Being bullied is not only hurtful, it's scary, too. Unfortunately, many kids go through the trauma of being targeted by a bully at home. Knowing what to do when bullied is crucial. There are specific words and actions to use to stay safe and end the abuse. Staying calm and simply telling the bully to stop is sometimes enough, but if not, remember that bullying usually happens because of the bully's insecurities or unhappiness. If dealing with siblings or parents who bully, just asking if they had a rough day might help them to take a step back and think about how their mood is affecting their words and actions. In some situations, walking or running away is the best thing to do to stay safe, even if that means running to a neighbor's house. Whatever happens in the moment, it's important to reach out for help afterwards. Leaning on friends and family members outside the home for support and reporting the bully to a trusted adult is essential. It's not easy to do this when the bully is a parent, but as long as a bully's behavior goes unchecked, it will continue. Remember that a bully's hurtful words are not true, even if they come from a parent. Bullies want to feel powerful and in control, and they rely on being able to intimidate others into keeping quiet. Usually, when they no longer have power or control, the bullying behaviors stop.

STANDING UP FOR A FRIEND OR SIBLING

Studies have shown that more than 50 percent of the time, interrupting a bully is enough to stop the bullying incident. It's important to know how to protect others from a bully without putting oneself in harm's way. Signe Whitson is a certified school social worker, a national educator on bullying prevention, and an expert in emotional and behavioral health in children and adolescents. She has some great tips to help kids stand up for friends or loved ones who are being bullied. According to Whitson, a simple statement that can be used at the first sign of bullying, such as "Hey, that's over the line" or "Cut it out, dude, that's not cool!," can be effective when it's a peer or sibling doing the bullying. If the bully is a parent, or if it just feels too risky to confront the bully in that way, another good strategy is to shift the bully's focus by asking a question. Examples of this are asking when a test or sporting event will be or what the score of a recent game was. Other strategies include saying someone is coming, telling a joke to lighten the mood, or walking right up to the person being bullied

Imagine a world in which everyone who witnessed bullying said or did something about it. Very quickly, we would have a world with no more bullies!

and standing close to him or her. Another good option is to walk away and quickly alert an adult outside the home. These are all strategies to use in the moment and must be followed up by encouraging the friend or sibling to seek help to stop the bullying at home.

ANTIBULLYING LAWS AND POLICIES

As of 2015, all fifty states in the United States have antibullying laws. In most states, the law stipulates that public schools must engage in an antibullying program. Unfortunately, this is very hard to enforce, and opinions vary on whether or not school programs have made a significant impact on bullying. School programs offer some helpful strategies and contact information for organizations that can help, but kids being bullied at home may not think the information applies to them. However, school officials and antibullying organizations can answer questions and offer assistance for kids who are bullied at home as well as at school. There's no doubt that public awareness of all types of bullying is higher than ever before, and there are many resources now available to victims of bullying.

Kids who are bullied at home face a unique set of challenges, but there are individuals and organizations ready to assist those in need. A school counselor, adult relative, teacher, pastor, or youth leader can help, and in a dangerous situation, never hesitate to call an emergency number, such as 911 in the United States. Speaking up, reaching out for help, and spreading kindness and compassion are the best ways to put an end to bullying, once and for all.

10 GREAT QUESTIONS

TO ASK A TRUSTED ADULT

1. How can I tell if I'm being bullied?

2. If I'm being bullied by a sibling, what should I do?

3. Why would a family member bully me?

4. What should I do if my parent is the bully?

5. If I say that my parent is bullying me, will I be taken away from my family?

6. If I tell my parents someone is bullying me and they don't believe me, what can I do?

7. Is there a number I can call to talk to someone anonymously about my situation?

8. Whom should I call if I'm in danger?

9. Should I try to fight someone who is bullying me?

10. What should I do if I know a friend is being bullied at home?

GLOSSARY

ACCOUNTABLE Responsible, as in, to be held responsible for something.

ANXIETY A long-term, chronic issue where a person deals with fear or worry that can affect their job performance or personal relationships.

BELITTLED Insulted or put down verbally and caused to feel inferior or ashamed.

BENIGN Not harmful; innocent.

BYSTANDER Someone who is present during something; a witness who does not engage in something that is happening.

COMPASSION Understanding others' suffering, feeling sympathy, and wanting to help.

CONDONED Accepted, allowed, or approved.

EMPATHY The understanding of someone else's feelings.

EVOLVED Changed gradually from simple to more complex, mature, or progressive.

EXCLUSION Being left out of something.

IMMUNE Unaffected or protected from the effects of something.

IMPLEMENTING Putting a plan into effect.

INFERIOR Lower in status or quality.

INTENTION Purpose or objective.

INTERVENE To act as an obstacle to prevent something from happening.

MALICIOUS Intending harm.

PERCEIVED To have realized or become aware of something.

RANDOM Unexpected; happening or being chosen without being planned.

REFUGE A shelter from harm; safe place.

TIRELESSLY With a lot of effort and hard work; exerting effort continuously or for a long time.

TRAUMATIC Very damaging and upsetting emotionally or psychologically.

FOR MORE INFORMATION

Kids Help Phone

789 W Pender Street, #570
Vancouver, BC V6C 1H2
Canada
(800) 668-6868
Website: https://kidshelpphone.ca
Facebook, Instagram, and Twitter: @kidshelpphone

Kids Help Phone is a Canadian organization that offers 24/7 help for young people dealing with complex issues such as abuse and bullying. Their site offers helpful articles, quizzes, and a Q&A section, as well as a direct number that youth can call, anonymously, to speak directly with a counselor.

PACER Center's Teens Against Bullying

8161 Normandale Boulevard
Minneapolis, MN 55437
(952) 838-9000
Website: https://pacerteensagainstbullying.org
Facebook: @Pacersnationalbullyingpreventioncenter
Instagram: @pacer_nbpc

The Teens Against Bullying program was created by PACER's National Bullying Prevention Center. Their site offers resources to help teens learn about, get support for, and take action against bullying.

PREVNet
Queen's University
100 Barrie Street
Kingston, ON K7L 3N6
Canada
(613) 533-2632
Website: https://www.prevnet.ca
Facebook, Instagram, Twitter: @prevnet

PREVNet is a Canadian organization dedicated to ending bullying. Their site provides data compiled by researchers and organizations at the forefront of the bullying prevention movement, including helpful resources and information about conferences, events, projects, and tips for bullying prevention.

Promote Prevent
Education Development Center, Inc.
43 Foundry Avenue
Waltham, MA 02453-8313
(617) 969-7100
Website: http://www.promoteprevent.org
Facebook and Instagram: @promoteprevent

PromotePrevent is an organization developed by the global nonprofit Education Development Center, Inc. Their goal is to promote safe and healthy schools and communities, where issues like bullying and the mental health of children are addressed properly and effectively. Their site offers numerous resources to aid in preventing and ending bullying.

Stomp Out Bullying

220 E 57th Street
New York, NY 10022
(877) 602-8559
Website: https://www.stompoutbullying.org
Facebook and Twitter: @stompoutbullying
Instagram: @theofficialstompoutbullying

Stomp Out Bullying is a national antibullying organization for kids and teens. Their site provides a list of upcoming events as well as vital information about how to get help and how to give help to those suffering from bullying.

StopBullying.gov

US Department of Health and Human Services
200 Independence Avenue SW
Washington, DC 20201
(877) 696-6775
Website: https://www.stopbullying.gov
Facebook: @stopbullying.gov
Twitter: @stopbullyinggov

StopBullying.gov is an organization managed by the US Department of Health and Human Services. This site promotes the prevention of bullying by providing information about different types of bullying and on the effects of bullying as well as numerous resources for those who need help and the latest information about laws pertaining to bullying.

FOR FURTHER READING

Bazelon, Emily. *Sticks and Stones: Defeating the Culture of Bullying and Rediscovering the Power of Character and Empathy*. New York, NY: Random House, 2014.

Brezina, Corona. *Helping a Friend Who Is Being Bullied*. New York, NY: Rosen Publishing, 2017.

Charlton-Trujillo, E. E. *Fat Angie*. Somerville, MA: Candlewick Press, 2015.

Coloroso, Barbara. *Bully, the Bullied, and the Not-So-Innocent Bystander*. New York, NY: William Morrow, 2016.

Hopkins, Ellen. *Rumble*. New York, NY: Margaret K. McElderry Books, 2016.

Kamberg, Mary-Lane. *I Have Been Bullied. Now What?* New York, NY: Rosen Publishing, 2015.

MacCarald, Clara. *Beating Bullying at Home and in Your Community*. New York, NY: Rosen Publishing, 2017.

Mayrock, Aija. *The Survival Guide to Bullying: Written by a Teen*. New York, NY: Scholastic, Inc., 2015.

Medina, Meg. *Yaqui Delgado Wants to Kick Your Ass*. Somerville, MA: Candlewick Press, 2014.

Stewart, Gail B. *Teens and Bullying*. San Diego, CA: ReferencePoint Press, Inc., 2016.

BIBLIOGRAPHY

Cullen, Damian. "Readers on Sibling Bullying: 'My Brother Hated Me from My Birth—He's a Monster.'" *Irish Times*, January 5, 2018. http://www.irishtimes.com/life-and-style/health-family/readers-on-sibling-bullying-my-brother-hated-me-from-my-birth-he-s-a-monster-1.3345869.

Cullen, Damian. "Readers on Sibling Bullying: 'My Tormentor Was There Every Day . . . Waiting.'" *Irish Times*, January 15, 2018. http://www.irishtimes.com/life-and-style/health-family/readers-on-sibling-bullying-my-tormentor-was-there-every-day-waiting-1.3349842.

Gordon, Sherri. "7 Ways Parents Can Address Sibling Bullying." Verywellfamily, November 1, 2018. http://www.verywellfamily.com/ways-parents-can-address-sibling-bullying-460680.

Gordon, Sherri. "The Fine Line Between Bullying and Bad Behavior." Verywellfamily, February 28, 2018. http://www.verywellfamily.com/bullying-or-unkind-behavior-how-to-know-the-difference-460493.

Graham, Jennifer. "What Sibling Bullying Is Doing to Your Children's Health." Deseret News, May 24, 2016. http://www.deseretnews.com/article/865654908/The-effects-of-sibling-bullying-on-your-childs-health.html.

Hicks, Janet. "When Sibling Conflict Becomes Bullying." *Psychology Today*, July 12, 2018. http://www.psychologytoday.com/us/blog/raising-parents/201807/when-sibling-conflict-becomes-bullying.

Hyken, Russell. "How Bully Parents Erode Kids' Self-Esteem and Create Long-Lasting Damage." *U.S. News & World Report*, July 13, 2017. http://health.usnews.com/wellness/for-parents/articles/2017-07-13/how-bully-parents-erode-kids-self-esteem-and-create-long-lasting-damage.

Johnson, Brian D., and Laurie Berdahl. "Family Matters When It Comes to Becoming a Bully." *Psychology Today*, November 19, 2016. http://www.psychologytoday.com/us/blog /warning-signs-parents/201611/family-matters-when-it-comes -becoming-bully.

Malecki, Christine K., and Michelle K. Demaray. "5 Signs That Sibling Fighting May Be Bullying." *Psychology Today*, December 1, 2014. http://www.psychologytoday.com/us /blog/the-wide-wide-world-psychology/201412/5-signs -sibling-fighting-may-be-bullying.

O'Friel, Emma. "Sibling Bullying: Humiliated and Scorned by a Family Member . . . This Is Not Just 'Sibling Rivalry.'" *Irish Times*, January 2, 2018. http://www.irishtimes.com/life-and -style/health-family/sibling-bullying-humiliated-and-scorned -by-a-family-member-this-is-not-just-sibling-rivalry-1.3327426.

Perry, Philippa. "Why We Must Take Sibling Bullying Seriously." *Guardian*, September 9, 2014. http://www.theguardian .com/commentisfree/2014/sep/09/sibling-bullying-evidence -depression-parents.

Schmidt, Samantha. "After Months of Bullying, Her Parents Say, a 12-Year-Old New Jersey Girl Killed Herself. They Blame the School." *Washington Post*, August 4, 2017. http://www .washingtonpost.com/news/morning-mix/wp/2017/08/02 /after-months-of-bullying-a-12-year-old-new-jersey-girl-killed -herself-her-parents-blame-the-school/?noredirect=on&utm _term=.0e4f9996a1e4.

Seto, Colleen. "Is It Sibling Bullying? How to Tell When the Fighting Has Gone Too Far." *Today's Parent*, February 13, 2018. http://www.todaysparent.com/family/is-it-sibling -bullying-how-to-tell-when-the-fighting-has-gone-too-far.

Tansill-Suddath, Callie. "A New Study Found That Being Bullied By A Sibling May Have Serious Consequences In Adulthood." Bustle, December 17, 2018. http://www.bustle.com/p/people

-who-are-bullied-by-siblings-as-kids-may-be-up-to-three
-times-more-likely-to-develop-psychotic-disorders-8193937.

Wang, Amy B. "A Boy Shared the Pain of Being Bullied—Inspiring Thousands to Show Him Love." *Washington Post*, December 11, 2017. http://www.washingtonpost.com/news/inspired
-life/wp/2017/12/10/a-boy-shared-the-pain-of-being-bullied
-inspiring-thousands-to-show-him-love/?noredirect=on&utm
_term=.c6ff2a16dbd1.

Whitson, Signe. "8 Things Kids Can Say or Do to Stop Bullying." *Huffington Post*, January 1, 2018. http://www.huffingtonpost
.com/entry/8-things-kids-can-say-or-do-to-stop-bullying
_us_5a4ad6ffe4b0d86c803c7905.

Yagoda, Maria. "Lady Gaga, Bella Hadid, Priyanka Chopra & More Stars Who've Opened Up About the Bullying They Faced as Kids." *People*, October 9, 2018. http://people.com
/celebrity/bullying-rumer-willis-jessica-alba-jessica-simpson
-and-eva-mendes.

INDEX

ABOUT THE AUTHOR

Jessica Shaw holds a BA in psychology from Texas State University. She has worked in human services and as a preschool teacher, and, having seen the negative impact of bullying firsthand, she has a special interest in empowering kids and putting a stop to bullying behaviors. She writes nonfiction, fiction, and poetry for children and young adults, including standardized testing material and work appearing in numerous children's publications.

PHOTO CREDITS

Cover New Africa/Shutterstock.com; p. 5 Kevin Winter/Getty Images; p. 7 Weston Colton/Getty Images; p. 9 cloki/Shutterstock.com; p. 10 yacobchuk/iStock/Getty Images; pp. 13, 19 JGI/Jamie Grill/Getty Images; p. 14 Mahathir Mohd Yasin/Shutterstock.com; p. 16 Africa Studio/Shutterstock.com; p. 21 Amir Ridhwan/Shutterstock.com; p. 24 sdominick/Photodisc/Getty Images; p. 26 Jamie Hooper/ Shutterstock.com; p. 28 LightField Studios/Shutterstock.com; p. 30 Wavebreakmedia/iStock/Getty Images; p. 32 jaguarblanco/ iStock/Getty Images; p. 34 asiseeit/E+/Getty Images; cover and interior graphic elements Olgastocker/Shutterstock.com (diagonal pattern), Solomnikov/Shutterstock.com (splatters).

Design & Layout: Brian Garvey; Editor: Bethany Bryan; Photo Researcher: Sherri Jackson